A Thought From St Ignatius Loyola
for Each Day of the Year

Translated from the French
by
Miss Margaret A. Colton

New York, Cincinnati, and St Louis
Benziger Brothers
Printers to the Holy Apostolic See
Copyright, 1887, by Benziger Brothers

ISBN: 978-0-9769118-5-2

The Type in this book is the property of
St Athanasius Press and except for brief
excerpts, may not be reproduced in whole
or in part without permission in writing
from the publisher.

Printed and Bound in the United States of America

Published by:

St Athanasius Press
133 Slazing Rd
Potosi, WI 53820
1-608-763-4097
melwaller@gmail.com
http://www.stathanasiuspress.com

Email is the best way to reach us.

Check out our other titles at the end of the book!

Specializing in reprinting Catholic Classics!

Table of Contents

January 4

February 14

March 22

April 31

May 40

June 50

July 59

August 68

September 78

October 87

November 96

December 106

A Thought From St Ignatius for Each Day of the Year

January

1.

All for the greater glory of God. -St Ignatius repeats these words three hundred and seventy-six times in his Constitutions. -Saurez, de Relig., Vol. 4, Book 8, ch. 6, n. 1.

2.

Spiritual Exercises are all that I can conceive, feel, and understand to be the best in this life, either for the personal advancement of each one, or for the benefit, aid, and spiritual advantages that may be drawn from them for others. -Letter 10.

3.

If the devil tempts me by the thought of Divine Justice, I think of God's Mercy; if he tries to fill me with presumption by the thought of His Mercy, I think of His Justice. -Letter 8.

4.

One of the most admirable effects of Holy Communion is to help those who fall through weakness to rise again; it is much more profitable, then, to approach this Divine Sacrament often with love, respect, and confidence than to remain away through an excess of fear and scrupulousness. -Letter 21.

5.

Provided that humility and sweetness are lacking in you, the goodness of God will not fail to help you to fulfill, not only without repugnance, but even with joy, whatever promises you have made Him. -Letter on Obedience.

6.

What I wish above all is, that you busy yourselves in the pure love of Jesus Christ, in the desire for His Glory, and the salvation of souls which He has so dearly purchased. -Letter 50.

7.

One who is ill must not wish to do the work of a well man; let him compensate by moderation and patience, and not injure his health. -Nolarci.

8.

I love to see the good in health, the wicked ill; the former because they consecrate their strength to the glory of God, the latter for the excess of evil they return to Him. -Ribadeneira, Book 5, ch. 2.

9.

I ardently desire, and I ask you by the love and respect we bear to our Divine Master, that in our spiritual exercises we would remember one another. -Letter 14.

10.

I do not desire to see in superiors all the emotions of the soul, and above all those of anger, extinguished and entirely destroyed, but I want them perfectly subdued. -Life, Book 3, n. 46.

11.

One must wage war against his predominant passion and not retreat until, with God's help, he has been victorious. -Maffoei, Book 3. ch. 1.

12.

It is God's love for us whence flows all the bitterness as well as all the sweets of this life. -Letter 136.

13.

More determination is required to subdue

the interior man than to mortify the body; and to break one's will than to break one's bones. -Bartoli, Book 4.

14.

To use the members of a religious order for the service of God, to the violation of the rule, is to throw down a tree to gather its fruit. -Bartoli, Book 5, ch. 1.

15.

Lord! What do I desire or what can I desire but You? -Ribaden., Book 5, ch. 1.

16.

Let the apostolic man not forget himself: he has not come to handle gold, but mud; he cannot, therefore, watch himself too carefully, that he may not contract the leprosy of which he seeks to cure others. -Life, Book 2.

17.

The vigor with which you resist the enemy will be the measure of the reward which will follow the combat. -Ribaden., ch. 37.

18.

That we may not be misled by self-love in the management of our affairs, let us not consider them as our own but as affairs, let us not consider them as our own but as another's; partiality will thus give way to justice. -Bartoli.

19.

While the enemy sees us humble, he tries to inspire the mind with a false humility. -Letter 8.

20.

He who bears God in his heart, carries his paradise with him everywhere. -In Compend. Vitae.

21.

Behold how the teachings of our Lord and Saviour, the Eternal Wisdom, are rejected, His deeds forgotten, and the price of His precious Blood lost, in a measure, considering how few there are who seek their salvation. -Letter 50.

22.

As for joy, as little as one can have of it in this life, experience shows that it is not the idle who possess it, but those who are zealous in the service of God. -Letter 50.

23.

Man has been created to praise, honor, and serve the Lord his God, and in this way to save his soul; and everything else on earth exists for man to aid him to reach the end which God has marked out for him in creating him. He must, then, use things as long only as they conduct him to this end, and abstain from them whenever they turn him aside from it. -Spiritual Exercise.

24.

Very few men understand what God would do for them, if they would but give themselves entirely to Him. -Bartoli, Book 4.

25.

He is ungrateful beyond all expression, and in heart altogether wrong, who, in the face of God's benefits, benefits which cost Him so much, does not offer himself, and does not see the obligation he is under to devote himself entirely to the honor and glory of our Lord and Saviour. -Letter 50.

26.

It is not the finest wood that feeds the fire of Divine Love, but the wood of the Cross. -Bartoli, Book 1.

27.

All the honey that can be gathered from the flowers of this world has less sweetness that the vinegar and gall of Jesus Christ our Lord. -Bartoli.

28.

Happy are they who in this life prepare themselves to be judged and saved by Christ our Lord, who must judge us for eternity. -Letter 14.

29.

Love consists in an interchange of favors. To obtain the love of God, I will call to mind the favors I have received from Him. -Spiritual Exercises.

30.

He employs his time badly who recites long prayer, when he should use it to conquer his passions. -Life, Book 3, ch. 12.

31.

One great difficulty of indiscreet fervor is to freight our bark too much. It should not be empty, lest it be capsized by the storm of temptation; but to load it so that it runs aground is still worse. -Letter 50.

February

1.

If you promise to do something tomorrow, do it today. -Letter 19.

2.

Regard as a temptation, and as something suspicious, all that is suggested to you contrary to God or the spirit of your institute. -Nolarci.

3.

Progress in the various spiritual exercises is in proportion to the renunciation that one makes of his self-love, his will, and all his pleasures. -Spiritual Exercise.

4.

Before attacking a man, Satan seeks the weakest or least guarded point; then erects his battery, that he may carry his assault.

Bartoli, Book 4, pp. 2 and 3.

5.

God is generous; I receive from His hands what I have never received from the hands of man; and if I had received nothing from man, I would receive all from God. -Bartoli, Book 4, ch. 23.

6.

I leave it to your own judgment if it is not best to thus make answer to all earthly things: What do they profit man? Or to exclaim later, having gained nothing: What do they profit me? -Life, Book 2, n. 2.

7.

We ought to direct all our efforts to reach the end which we pursue, and once having entered on the way of perfection, strive to gain its highest point. -Lancicius.

8.

In the work of salvation, we must employ against the enemy the weapons with which he strives to destroy us. -History of the Society, Book 3.

9.

Arguments and human reasoning will never teach us as much as a humble recourse to God. -Nolarci.

10.

There is nothing of which apostolic men have more need than interior recollection, in order not to endanger their own salvation while seeking that of others. -Ribaden., Book 7.

11.

Put a limit to your prudence, for it is not necessary to carry to excess a virtue which should serve to rule and guide others. Ribadeneira.

12.

Our enemy waxes wroth when a soul discloses itself to a good confessor, or to some spiritual person who knows his cunning and wickedness, because he foresees that, his snares once discovered, he can no longer carry out his treacherous work. -Spiritual Exercise.

13.

Take it for a principle to concede readily in the beginning of a conversation with those whose aspirations are only earthly; but reserve yourself for the end and try to cover with a layer of gold the metal of their conversation, whatsoever it may be. -Bartoli, Book 4.

14.

A man whose heart is perverted would not know how to remain long among those who place their happiness in virtue. -Bartoli,

Book 6. ch. 37.

15.

It is not only necessary to consider what God's zeal requires in itself, but one must apply and use this zeal to the interest of his neighbor. -Ribaden., ch. 47

16.

Let the hope of one day doing great things in the service of God not make you neglect the present moment.

17.

It is better to be cut off from life, than to live for vanity. -Nolarci.

18.

Do not wait for old age to mortify your body and your passions. First, are you sure of reaching it? Again, how shall you do penance at that age? -Nolarci.

19.

You wish to reform the world, reform yourself, otherwise your efforts will be in vain. -Bartoli, Book 4.

20.

The value of a thing is only its worth before God. -Bartoli, Book 4, ch. 55.

21.

If God gives you much suffering, it is a sign that He wishes to make you a great Saint. -Bartoli, Book 4.

22.

Resolve never to do anything while moved by passion; wait until it passes away and then take counsel only after mature deliberation. -Of the Elect.

23.

Ask of God much suffering; in giving it to you, He will do you a great favor, for in this single gift are countless blessings. -Bartoli, Book 4.

24.

Among all the evils and all the sins, ingratitude is according to the best judgment, the most deserving of abhorrence on the part of God, our Lord and Creator, and of all the creatures worthy of His Divine and Eternal Glory. -Letter 24.

25.

It is obligatory on us to lead to Jesus Christ our Lord, by the most direct and surest path, those who live under the same roof with us. -Letter 34.

26.

Let us proceed joyfully and let us be sure that all our crosses will bear Christ with

them, and that His help, which will never be wanting to us, will be more powerful than the combined efforts of all our enemies.
-Bartoli, Book 2.

27.

I commend to you devotion in helping your neighbor's soul in such a manner, that you always have a care of your own, to preserve and perfect it in every kind of virtue to the glory of the Lord our God. -Letter 151.

28.

It is part of Divine Goodness to defend with greater solicitude that which the devil attacks with most ardor. -History of the Society, p. 1.

MARCH

1.

They who are engage with the salvation of their neighbor, will gain more by a humble modesty than by an authoritative manner, and will gain victory sooner in retreat than in combat. -Life, Book 4.

2.

Too much hatred of our neighbor's faults begets more aversion than amendment, and, far from helping him, puts him to flight. -Abridgment of his Life.

3.

One does not speak of the works of God, even with the least of mortals, without drawing great profit from it. -Nolarci.

4.

By preference, the devil attacks man at the

moment of awaking; before the mind has had time to pious thoughts, he presents to it bad and forbidden ones. -Ribadeneira, ch. 37.

5.

Even among the present hardships of our exile, and the weariness of our pilgrimage, obedience gives us a foretaste of our heavenly country. -Letter 51.

6.

It is an extreme punishment that obliges us to remain so long on earth, unless love causes us to live more in Heaven and with God than on earth and with ourselves; just as the rays of the sun continue to shed their light a great way off as long as they are not separated from their focus. -Bartoli, Book 4.

7.

How few there are who avail themselves of the precious blood of Jesus to purchase their salvation! -Bartoli, Book 4.

8.

Though the world could give you, in an instant, the most enticing thing of all that it offers, and let you see, at a glance, all the kingdoms of the earth, and all their glory, could you possess them beyond the short time of your life? -Bartoli, Book 2.

9.

In our ministry to men, we must imitate the angels; they do not neglect any means to procure their salvation, but the result, whether good or bad, causes them to lose nothing of their blessed and eternal peace. -Ribadeneira, Book 5. c. 2.

10.

You must avoid every vice, but above all those which tempt you most: it is in these you will find your greatest danger, if you do not take wise precautions. Ribadeneira, ch.

37.

11.

If one fears men much he will never do anything great for God: all that one does for God arouses persecution. -Bartoli.

12.

Just as we drive out one nail by another, let us oppose effort to effort, habit to habit. -Maffoei.

13.

All creatures are at the service of God's friends; they help them to acquire greater merit to attach and unite themselves by a closer affection to their Creator. -Letter 34.

14.

With Divine consolation all troubles change into pleasures, all weariness into rest. For whoever advances with this interior peace, is never so burdened but that it feels light. -Letter 8.

15.

He who has renounced the world or despises it should resemble a statue which does not prevent itself being dressed in rags, nor being despoiled of the purple which ornaments it. -Lancicius.

16.

It is not enough to say you desire to serve our Lord: you must declare and acknowledge fearlessly that you are His servant and His slave, and that you would die rather than abandon His service. -Letter 8.

17.

The infernal enemy never has more power against you than when he acts secretly. -Spiritual Exercises.

18.

When the enemy cannot succeed in making you sin, and has lost the hope of attaining this end, he strives at least to torment you. -Letter 4.

19.

One ought not to abstain from the Bread of Angels, because he does not feel his sentiments loving enough; that would be to wish to die of hunger because one has not honey. -Life, Book 4.

20.

It is no less a miracle to see a religious sad, seeking God alone, than to see true joy in him who seeks all outside of God. -Trinkel in Exerc.

21.

They who live under the rule of obedience have necessarily all the more opportunity to advance in perfection, either because God, who is the Author of perfection, hears their prayers or because, as a wise man has said: "All that man retrenches from his own will he adds to his perfection". -Letter 51.

22.

A precious crown is reserved in Heaven for those who perform all their actions with all the diligence of which they are capable; for it is not sufficient to do our part well, it must be done more than well. -Nolarci.

23.

I will carefully consider how, on the day of judgment, I would wish to have discharged my office or my duty; and the way I would wish to have done it then, I shall do now. -Spiritual Exercises.

24.

It is much better to obtain only an ounce of happiness in not risking our salvation, then one hundred pounds in hazarding it. -Bartoli, Book 4, ch. 35.

25.

It is a great source of joy for Satan to see a soul rushing on heedlessly and deaf to the warnings which would restrain it; for as much as its pretensions are exaggerated, so great will be its fall. -Nolarci.

26.

One should neither do nor write anything from which hatred or bitterness may arise. -Maffoei.

27.

In order that a correction may be administered with fruit, authority must be in the one giving it, and love in the one receiving it. -Bartoli.

28.

The only lawful ambition is to love God and the price of this love is to love Him more. -Bartoli, Book 4.

29.

A religious ought to dread more, being afraid of poverty than experiencing it. -Bartoli.

30.

Obedience will open for us, beyond a doubt, the portals of Heaven, which were formerly closed against us by the breaking of a Divine Commandment, and which still are shut to whomsoever is guilty of the same crime. -Letter 51.

31.

I call those thoughts mean which, in spite of the vain efforts to prolong them, can only last for a short space of time; I call those despicable which extend not beyond this earth. -Bartoli, Book 2.

APRIL

1.

You should bring to your praiseworthy exercises a holy fervor, because you will feel, even in this life, its good effects, not only in perfecting your souls, but also in the peace of mind you will possess. -Letter 50.

2.

There are two guarantees of a wise rule of conduct: thought before action, and self-command afterwards. -Martini

3.

If you possess any temporal good, be not a slave to it, but give glory to the Sovereign Master, from whom you have everything. -Letter 11.

4.

If the love of God burns in your heart, you

will understand that to suffer for God is a joy to which all earthly pleasures are not to be compared. -Bartoli, Vol. 1, p. 107.

5.

Why so much fatigue to procure earthly happiness for a soul whose origin is heavenly, a transient glory for a soul capable of loving and enjoying God Himself forever? -Bartoli, Vol. 1, p. 126.

6.

They who aspire to reform the morals of others lose their time and their pains, by not preaching by example, in correcting themselves first. -Bartoli, Book 4.

7.

You should always manage, as far as in you lies, that no one may depart after your sermon less disposed to peace with God than he was before it. -Instruction to Fathers Laynez and Salmeron.

8.

If we do not feel within us a perfect patience, we have more reason to pity the grossness of our nature for being neither mortified nor dead to the things of this world, as we should be, than to blame those who load us with insults and ignominy. -Letter 4.

9.

We should not fear much the insults of this life, which are confined to words; were they all united they could not hurt a hair of our head. -Letter 4.

10.

When the object of our love is infinite we can always love more and more. -Letter of April 15, 1543.

11.

The acknowledgment of and gratitude for favors and gifts received is loved and esteemed in Heaven and on earth. -Letter 34.

12.

The first temptation is riches, the second honors, the third pride, and by these three degrees Satan leads us to all other vices. -Spiritual Exercises.

13.

In the servants of God it is not the numbers I seek but the merit; I like better to see them distinguish themselves by their deeds than by their name or habit. -History of the Society. Book 1.

14.

Outside of the Church there is nothing truly good; for whoever will not be united to this mystic body, will not receive from the Head, who is Christ Jesus, the Divine grace which invigorates the soul and prepares it for eternal happiness. -Letter 152.

15.

If charity and sweetness have not truth for their companion they do not deserve the names of charity and sweetness, but those of hypocrisy and vanity. -Bartoli, Book 4.

16.

In scientific matters there is a manifest difference between the studious and the negligent man; now, this difference is the same regarding progress in virtue and victory over the weakness of our nature. -Letter 50.

17.

One ought to speak little and hear much. -Bartoli, Book 4.

18.

In every occupation obedience will help you

to advance with increasing merit in the way of perfection, like those who are navigating: for even when resting they are still sailing onward. -Letter 51.

19.

He who cannot make up his mind to give up all for Christ ought at least to refer all to Him; and to consider the highest honors as infinitely inferior to that one only thing which our Lord and Saviour has declared necessary. -Bartoli.

20.

Is this world, where God has placed you, a Heaven and not a veritable hell? Or is it so very easy to escape that it is not even necessary to think of it? -Letters.

21.

According as you form a closer union and friendship with spiritual men, you will enjoy more happiness in the Lord. -Orland, Book

5, n. 110.

22.

In the face of the never ceasing snares of the enemy, it is necessary to have each day a fixed hour for review, to enter into one's self and consider carefully, in presence of God, all one's thoughts, words, and actions. -Lyr.

23.

Imperfect obedience has eyes for its misfortunes; perfect obedience is wisely blind; the first passes judgment on the orders it receives, the second lays aside all judgment. -Ribadeneira, ch. 33.

24.

I call consolation every increase of faith, hope, and charity, all interior joy which summons and animates man to desire heavenly things, and to wish for his soul's salvation; in fine, all that which brings to it repose and peace in its Lord and Maker.

-Spiritual Exercises.

25.

Were you to live a hundred years the possessor of all the kingdoms of the earth and all their glory, will not the last day, the last hour finally come for you? And if you, the possessor for a day of a portion considerably less, were deprived of God for an eternity, would you gain by the exchange? -Bartoli, Book 2.

26.

All ought to make the holy will of God the center and lever of all their actions, and His Divine qualities the only object of their discourse, the only end of their hopes. -Summary of Constitutions.

27.

In order to combat desolation and put temptation to flight, one ought to persevere in prayer a little beyond the prescribed time.

Thus he will accustom himself not only to resist the enemy, but to overthrow him. -Spiritual Exercises.

28.

They who, by a generous effort, make up their minds to obey, acquire great merit; for obedience by its sacrifices resembles martyrdom. -Letter 50.

29.

By the love and respect we owe to Jesus Christ our Lord, I beg of you to begin without delay to amend your lives with the greatest care, so that at the last day, when it will be necessary to give an exact account of them, you will be found worthy. -Letter 13.

30.

In the spiritual life no storm is more formidable than calmness itself, nor an adversary more dangerous than the absence of adversaries. -Bartoli, Book 2, ch. 18.

MAY

1.

Before determining on an enterprise we should offer it to God, seeing that success must come only from Him; nevertheless, in the choice of means and by constant efforts, work as if the entire success depended altogether on ourselves. -Bartoli, Vol. 2, p. 955.

2.

God takes particular care to detach those from the fleeting pleasure of this life whom He loves a love of predilection, by the desire with which He inspires them for the heavenly life, and by the grief and afflictions which He sends them in this life. -Letter 432.

3.

Nothing created can bring to the soul joy equal to that of the Holy Ghost.

-Ribadeneira, Book 5. ch. 10.

4.

In your dress permit nothing unclean or slovenly, but at the same time avoid a studied elegance, which is not free from daintiness or affectation. -Bartoli, Book 4.

5.

If you wish to end your undertakings happily, learn how to give yourself up to them without desiring any return to yourself. -Ribadeneira, Book 5, ch. 2.

6.

Among those who are united in our Lord Jesus Christ by the bonds of charity, and by the desire to procure the honor and glory of God, the most profitable words are those which the Holy Ghost engraves on their hearts by the prayers which they offer for one another. -Letter 64.

7.

Do nothing, say nothing before considering if that which you are about to say or do is pleasing to God, profitable to yourself, and edifying to your neighbor. -Lyr.

8.

If we were to place on one side of a scale all the good things created by God, and on the other side all the prisons with all their terrors, the galleys with all their ignominies, the former would in no way counter balance the latter. -Ribaden., Book 5, ch. 10.

9.

Be ready to serve those who are lest able to help themselves, for the courtier, to gain the favor of an earthly prince, will often serve him more faithfully than you serve the King of Heaven. -Letter 50.

10.

Our enemy employs no surer artifice for banishing true charity from the hearts of God's servants, than to make them rule themselves in spiritual matters, not with calmness and reason, but thoughtlessly and with all the unrestrained violence of their passions. -Letter 50.

11.

When we compare our condition with that of our brethren in India, I cannot see that ours is a hard lot. -Letter 114.

12.

In dryness as well as in consolations, dangers are encountered if one is not on his guard; if the latter can inspire pride, the former can beget tepidity.

13.

Go and set the whole world on fire with the Divine Love. -Card. Lud.

14.

We should not only turn our thoughts to Heaven in prayer, but we should accustom ourselves to behold God in everything.
-Life, Book 5.

15.

Meditation and intercourse with God restrain the violence of our unruly nature, and keep its follies within bounds. -Lyr.

16.

When one reads a good work by a dangerous author, first the book pleases, then the author himself; from that moment, finding the mind predisposed in his favor, he easily inculcates his deadly principles. -Ribadeneira, ch. 35.

17.

It is the tactics of the devil to attack a man from without rather than within; God, on the contrary, rather moves and forms interiorly.

-Bartoli, Book 4.

18.

They who at the outset count up too strictly the difficulties and accidents of an undertaking, or who yield to fear too easily, will never accomplish anything great. -Ribadeneira, ch. 37.

19.

If only a child profits by my teachings, my trouble and my time will seem to me well spent. -Bartoli, Vol. 2, p. 142

20.

It is by acting contrary to the suggestions of the enemy that we will not be deceived, and that the deceiver will be deceived himself. -Letter 8.

21.

In treating with men we must speak little

and hear much; and speak even these few words as if the whole world were to hear them, though we speak only to one. -Bartoli, Vol. 2, p. 254.

22.

In loving God for Himself, and man for God, one does what the law commands him, following the sayings of St Paul: "He that loves his neighbor has fulfilled the law." (Romans 13:8) And indeed, by this very charity which animates him towards his neighbor, he loves God and man at the same time, with the same love. -Letter 16.

23.

There is no doubt that God will never be wanting to us, provided that He finds in us that humility which makes us worthy of His gifts, the desire of possessing them, and the promptitude to cooperate industriously with the graces He gives us. -Letter 50.

24.

Lord, take and receive all my liberty, my memory, my understanding, and my entire will, all that I have and all that I may possess. You have given me all, Lord, I return all to You; all is Yours. Do with pleasure. Give me Your love and Your grace, these are sufficient for me. -Spiritual Exercises.

25.

Whoever desires to act and live in peace among men, ought to try, above all, to be good to everyone, and injure no one. -Orland, Book 5, n. 24.

26.

Alas! How vile the earth appears to me, when I contemplate Heaven! -Bartoli, Book 4, ch. 28.

27.

God gives to each one of us sufficient grace

ever to know His holy will and to do it fully.
-End of St Ignatius' Letters.

28.

Wicked or misinformed men may calumniate you; pray to God that it may never come to pass that any one may speak any evil of you that is not a calumny.
-Bartoli.

29.

Let him who finds himself desolate remember how strong he is by grace, which is sufficient to enable him to overcome all his enemies, and that he should take courage in his Lord and Creator. -Spiritual Exercises.

30.

Place before your eyes as models for imitation, not the weak and cowardly, but the fervent and courageous. -Letter 50.

31.

To conquer himself is the grandest victory that man can gain. -Letter 51.

JUNE

1.

The despising of one's self in the midst of honors and riches, and disdain for all glory, should be esteemed more highly than corporal mortification. -Bartoli.

2.

The shortest way, yes, the only way to reach sanctity, is to conceive a horror for all that the world loves and values. -Examination, ch. 4.

3.

It would be the greatest miracle to see God deny His help to those who, for love of Him, have given up everything. -Bartoli, Book 4.

4.

You must practice, at one and the same time, interior and exterior mortification;

but with the difference, that you must give yourself up to the first particularly, always, and without exception; to the second, on the contrary, only as far as circumstances and the particular condition of persons and the occasions will permit. -Bartoli, Book 3.

5.

The poison which is found in books soon infects the whole mind, if one does not check it from the first. -Ribadeneira, Book 5, ch. 10.

6.

We should ask ourselves at the very outset of our lives, this: What will God exact of us on judgment day? What account must we render? So that we may have for our rule of conduct His judgment, and not our fancy. -Life, Book 5.

7.

God inclines to shower His graces upon

us, but our perverted will is a barrier to His generosity. -Bartoli.

8.

It seems to me that the Divine and Sovereign Goodness wishes to give you in His Kingdom a most plentiful and munificent reward for the service you render Him; since for the good deeds for which others receive at least a little consolation in return, even as regards man, you have known only pain and most extraordinary contradictions. -Letter 172.

9.

When God shall have wholly occupied our souls in spite of ourselves, since no one can rob us of our Divine Treasure, there is nothing in the daily occurrence of this life which ought to grieve or worry us much, for every affliction, whatsoever may be the cause, only comes from the loss of an object that one loves, or from the fear of losing it. -Letters.

10.

If we confide in God's providence and resign ourselves entirely into His hands, and renounce our individual pleasure, He is pleased to reward us with great peace and interior consolation, and all the more so if we seek ourselves less, and more purely desire the Divine Glory and God's good pleasure. -Letter 139.

11.

The cowardly, for not wishing to fight against themselves, will never enjoy, or only late, true peace of soul and the possession of any perfection; the brave and the earnest possess both in a short time. -St Ignatius.

12.

We do not always rejoice in consolations; but all is for our good, whether God gives or denies it. -Letter 8.

13.

Be assured that in the study of perfection, as in that of the sciences, any act animated by holy fervor makes more progress than a thousand others produced by sloth; so that what the careless man acquires with trouble, after many years, the fervent man readily obtains in a short time. -Letter 50.

14.

God's way in dealing with those whom He intends to admit the soonest after this life into the possession of His everlasting glory, is to purify them in this world by the greatest afflictions and trials. -Letter 126.

15.

If you wish to advance in the love of God, speak of it; for pious conversations are to charity what the wind is to the flame. -Letter of April 15, 1543

16.

He who forgets himself in the service of God may be assured that God will not forget him. -Bartoli, Vol. 2, p. 254.

17.

All that you say in secret, speak as if you were addressing a multitude. -Nolarci.

18.

If you look into it, you will see that in times past, when you fell into many sins, and were less desirous to serve our Lord, you were neither tempted nor troubled as much by this serpent, who is ever seeking to disturb us. For then your mode of life pleased him, while now he cannot endure the change in you. -Letter 13.

19.

Although it is sovereignly praiseworthy and useful to serve God by pure love, we should not less earnestly commend the fear of His

Divine Majesty. -Spiritual Exercises.

20.

Hold any man's salvation at greater value than all the treasures of the world. -Ribaden., Book 5, ch. 8.

21.

It is part of the father of lies to speak of or devise one or more truths, only to end by an imposture, that he may entrap us into sin. -Letter 66.

22.

If, after we have commenced the practice of virtue, we begin to fear and lose heart because of the temptations we experience, no beast on earth becomes so ferocious as the enemy of our souls, so deep is the hatred with which he pursues his wicked designs. -Spiritual Exercises.

23.

Once our motives are pure and upright, and we seek not our interests, but those of our Lord and Master, He has a constant care over us because He is infinitely good. -Letter 117.

24.

To use profitably for our neighbor's salvation the gifts nature has given us, they must be actuated from within and draw their strength there from. -Bartoli, Book 4.

25.

We should not measure our spiritual progress by our deeds, our amiability, or our love of solitude, but by the violence we do ourselves. -Maffoei.

26.

The successful seeker of souls must feign blindness of many things; for once master of the will, he can lead as he pleases those who practice virtue under his guidance. -Bartoli, Book 4.

27.

That which would have been easily remedied at first becomes incurable by time and habit. -Bartoli.

28.

Men of great virtue, though of meager knowledge, incite men more effectively to virtuous lives by their words and example, than the greatest masters of eloquence. -Bartoli.

29.

The whole life of religious Orders depends upon the preservation of their first spirit. -Orland, Book 6.

30.
Be diffident; how powerful is confidence in God! -Ribadeneira, ch. 36.

JULY

1.

Do you wish to be always happy? Then always be humble and obedient. -A. Costerus.

2.

It is characteristic of God and of His angels to bring to the soul, when they occupy it, true happiness and spiritual joy; and to drive from it the sadness and trials which the enemy incites in it. -Spiritual Exercises.

3.

One difficulty of indiscreet fervor is that far from subduing the old man, it subdues the new; that is to say, it weakens and renders him incapable of practicing virtue. -Letter 50.

4.

He who wishes to reach the highest point of perfection must begin at the lowest; the height of perfection is in proportion to the depth of its roots; and is higher and higher as its roots are deeper. -Bartoli.

5.

To serve the servants of my Lord is my honor and my glory. -Letter 3.

6.

We must not speak an idle word, that is to say, a word which is not useful, either to ourselves, our neighbor, or directed to that end. -Spiritual Exercises.

7.

Prudence is not the virtue of him who obeys, but of him who commands; the only way to act prudently in obeying is to give up prudence sooner than cease to be obedient. -Bartoli.

8.

There is not a sacrifice sweeter or more agreeable to God than obedience. Obedience is better than sacrifice, says the Scripture. -Letter 51.

9.

Among the gifts of grace which the soul receives in Holy Communion, there is one that must be counted among the highest; it is that Holy Communion does not permit the soul to remain long in sin, nor to obstinately persevere in it. -Letter 34.

10.

Do not put faith in constant happiness, and fear most when all smiles upon you. -History of the Society, Book 14, 9.

11.

If anyone asks you for something that you believe would be injurious to him, refuse, but in such a manner as not to lose his good will. -Nolarci.

12.

What have I done for Christ? What am I doing for Christ? What ought I to do for Christ, my Lord and Saviour? -Spiritual Exercises.

13.

Nothing should influence me to one decision more than another, unless the service and glory of the Lord my God, and the eternal salvation of my soul. -Spiritual Exercises.

14.

Let superiors take care not to estrange their subordinates by severity; even a suspicion of it does harm. -Bartoli, Book 3.

15.

Pursue with invincible courage the end

to which you have been called; God has furnished such help and means to aid you in attaining it. -Bartoli, Book 4.

16.

A soul who desires to make progress in the spiritual life should always act contrary to the enemy. -Spiritual Exercises.

17.

Obedience not only makes us enjoy repose, but it ennobles and raises man above his state; it cause him to put off himself and to put on Christ, the Sovereign Good, who is accustomed to fill all the more that soul which He finds least taken up with itself; in fine, those who have reached this state have a true right to pronounce these words of the Apostle: "I live, now not I, but Christ lives in me." -Letter 51.

18.

I am persuaded that a servant of God

recovered from illness is cured, partly in order that he may direct and arrange all the acts of his life to the glory of God, our adorable Master. -Letter 4.

19.

Alas! How men deceive themselves, who thinking they are spiritual, seek to guide souls! -Bartoli, Book 4.

20.

A quarter of an hour's meditation does more for a man who has conquered himself, that one of several hours for a man still unsubdued. -Ribadeneira.

21.

If our natural feelings, being hurt, cause us to utter some words, or to act in opposition with the principles we profess, we must chastise them severely until they have obeyed us. -Bartoli, Book 3.

22.

The more a soul enjoys peace and solitude, the more apt it is to seek and find its Creator. -Spiritual Exercises.

23.

Here is the difference between the joys of the world and the Cross of Jesus Christ; after having tasted the first, one is disgusted with them and on the contrary, the more one partakes of the Cross the greater the thirst for it. -Ribadeneira.

24.

A great help to advancement in spiritual life is to have a friend whom you will permit to inform you of your faults. -Life

25.

He who has recourse to God, so that He may enlighten him on whatever he asks of Him, whether for a choice of state of life, or for any other spiritual interest, ought first to lay aside his own will and preference, then place himself unreservedly in the hands of the Divine Majesty, with a full determination of accomplishing whatsoever His holy will may make known to him. -Bartoli, Book 4.

26.

The apostolic laborer ought to suit himself to every character: at first, he should feign and kindly forbear with many things; but once he has obtained the good will of those with whom he is dealing, he should attack them with their own weapons. -Ribaden., ch. 37.

27.

If you earnestly desire to mortify yourself in youth, let it be in breaking your will, and subjecting your private judgment to the control of obedience, rather than in weakening and wounding your body by excesses. -Letter 50.

28.
Oh, my God! Oh! If men but knew You, they would never offend You! -Life.

29.

The true peace of God, penetrating the depth of the soul, brings with it every help and grace necessary to secure its salvation and reach eternal life. -Letter 15.

30.

One does not conquer his anger by flying the cause, but by fighting it. Solitude does not do away with impatience, but only conceals it. -Bartoli, Vol. 2, p. 176.

31.
We should express ourselves in few words; the truth is all its simplicity suffices. We should guard against enlarging on the consequences; truth in itself always carries conviction; too many ornaments but weaken and over weight it in its struggle with error. -Bartoli, Vol. 2, p. 127.

AUGUST

1.

If God could not be with us on our altars to expand more and more freely, day after day, the sources of His Mercy, Jesus Christ, His only Son, would not exhort us to undertake what His powerful arm alone can aid us to accomplish, when He tells us: "Be you perfect as My heavenly Father is perfect." -Letter 50.

2.

They who labor in God's vineyard ought to have, as it were, only one foot resting on earth, the other continually raised to walk in the way of our Lord. -Rev. Goser. Michel

3.

Our Lady, deign to intercede for us sinners with thy Divine Lord and Son, and obtain of Him a blessing for us in our trials and tribulations. -Letter 1.

4.

I admire those who live in community and have a care over one another in mutual remembrance, who are lost to self, that they may be one in God their Creator. -Letter 34.

5.

Take care that the worldings do not pursue with greater care and anxiety the perishable goods of this world, than you do the eternal. -Letter on Perfection.

6.

One should know, before entering the religious life, that he will not remain there, nor find peace, unless he crosses the threshold with his feet tied, that is, unless he makes a sacrifice of his will and judgment. -Bartoli, Book 3.

7.

It is not enough to love our own souls, we must have love for all mankind. -Bartoli, Book 4.

8.

To deserve the name of a true religious, it is not only necessary to renounce the world, but still more to renounce one's self. -Bartoli, Book 3.

9.

In correcting any one, should kindness fail, use severity, that it may be useful, at least to others. -Ribadeneira, Book 5, ch. 7.

10.

A crooked and rough trunk of a tree, if it could think, would never believe that it could become a statue, a masterpiece of sculpture: it would not wish to place itself under the chisel of anyone who by his art, sees well what he could make of it. Thus many people, hardly living as Christians, are far from imagining that they could become great Saints, if they allowed the grace of God to act in them and not resist its influence. -Bartoli, Book 4.

11.

It is very dangerous to wish to lead everyone to perfection by the same path; it is not known how numerous and varied are the gifts of the Holy Ghost. -Quartemius.

12.

I do not know a greater happiness than to die for Jesus Christ, or for the salvation of my neighbor. Nadasi.

13.

If men but knew You, O my God! -Life, Book 4, ch. 28.

14.

As they who endeavor to drive away a

bad thought deserve a great reward from Heaven, in the same way they who resist holy inspirations expose themselves to the danger of falling into the greatest sins. -Nolarci.

15.

Self-love sometimes obscures the light of intelligence in such a manner that it makes us consider as impossibilities what in more lucid moments appear not only easy, but even necessary. -Bartoli.

16.

The devil, who has not power over the soul, is often the author of fanciful imaginations, and uses the body to mislead the souls of such as are naturally vain and fond of novelties. -Ribaden., ch. 37.

17.

We must sail against wind and tide, and hope the more as all appears more desperate.

-Bartoli, Vol. 3, p. 213.

18.

Any tempest which assails us and which we did not bring on ourselves through any fault of ours, foretells a consolation soon to follow it. -History of the Society, Book 2, p. 1.

19.

In order that you may know how to command and govern others well, you must first be careful to obey, and excel in the science of obedience. -Letter 51.

20.

Love above everything the glory of God. May God, infinitely good, be the aim of your words, your thoughts, and your actions. -Letter 1.

21.

In speaking to the sad and sore of heart present to them a cheerful and serene countenance; speak with all sweetness, so as to restore them the more easily to peace and tranquility, overcoming in this way one extreme by another. -Instruction to Fathers Salmeron and Broet.

22.

One ought to obey a superior, not on account of his wisdom, goodness, or other qualities which God had given him, but only because he is God's representative and acts by His authority, who has said: "He that hears you, hears Me; he that despises you, despises Me." -Letter on Obedience.

23.

For the love of our Lord let us make generous efforts in His holy service, since we are indebted to Him for so much; we will tire sooner in receiving His gifts, than will He is bestowing them. -Letter 1.

24.

Treat sinners as a good mother treats her sick child; she lavishes more caresses on him than when he is well. -Bartoli.

25.

In martyrdom only the desire to live is sacrificed, but in obedience every kind of desire is sacrificed at one and the same time. -Letter 51.

26.

May it please the Mother of God to hear the vow I make for you. On condition that you will have a patience and perfect constancy, and that there will be no sin on the part of others, I desire, then that you may receive a great many more humiliations, so that you may have constant opportunities of acquiring new merits. -Letter 4.

27.

Be careful and do not lightly condemn the actions of others; we must consider the intention of our neighbor, which is often good and pure, although the act itself seems blameworthy. -Bartoli, Book 4.

28.

God instructs us in a twofold manner: in the first He leads us Himself, but secretly, and therefore, unknown; in the second, it is man who leads us by His permission. -Bartoli, Book 4, ch. 22.

29.

Let us often say to ourselves that wherever we are, or wherever we may go, even if it be to India, our loss is not felt. -Letter 114.

30.

They who fulfill the orders of their superiors reluctantly and unwillingly should be classed among the vilest slaves. -Maffoei, Book 2, ch. 7.

31.

Vanity and vain glory are vices born of ignorance and blind self-love. -Life, Book 4, ch. 4.

SEPTEMBER

1.

Never believe an accuser until after you have found the accused and found him guilty. -Nolarci.

2.

It is an art as rare as it is precious, to transact business with many people, without ever forgetting one's self or God. -Quartemius.

3.

Virtue and holiness of life are not only all-powerful, or at least very powerful with God, but also with men. -Quartemius.

4.

They who shine by birth, learning, or other qualities, ought to excel in self-denial, otherwise they render themselves more culpable than men without nobility and learning. -Bartoli, Book 4.

5.

He who beholds Heaven with a pure eye, sees better the darkness of a earth; for, although the latter seems to have some brilliancy, it disappears before the splendor of the heavens. -Bartoli.

6.

One ought ardently to desire that charm of language so necessary in treating with men. -Life.

7.

I desire with ardor and more than ardor, if I may thus express myself, that the true love of God may become perfect in you, and that you may consecrate your strength to the service and glory of God our Master, so that I may be able to love and serve you more and more. -Letter 3.

8.

Oh, no! Your heart is not so narrow that the world can satisfy it entirely; nothing, nothing but God can fill it. -Bartoli, Book 2.

9.

If you attach your heart to certain places and occupations, obedience oftentimes places you in some other place that you may not like; to be always cheerful, be always humble and obedient. -Bartoli, Book 4.

10.

If, one day, I should offend God in any way, or grow remiss, though ever so little, in that which concerns His holy service and glory, I solemnly implore Him, rather let me die. -Letter 3.

11.

Obedience which ceases at the fulfilling of orders is bad and defective; it does not deserve the name of virtue if it does not rise higher, and make our will and that of our superior one and the same thing. -Letter on Obedience.

12.

Do not worry yourself over bad, obscene or carnal thoughts, nor about your afflictions or annoyances, when you experience them in spite of yourself. St Peter and St Paul were not able to avoid these trials in all, or even in part. -Letter 8.

13.

Everyone should try to have his heart always occupied and filled with God, to love Him and think of Him only, and whether alone or with others never to be out of His presence. -Bartoli, Vol. 2, p. 6.

14.

Idleness begets a discontented life; it develops self-love, which is the cause of all our misery, and renders us unworthy to receive the favors of Divine love. -Letter 10.

15.

The errors of others, the portion left our poor humanity, should serve to keep us from adding any of ours to them. -Ribadeneira.

16.

I do not wish, on my leaving this world, that there be found on me, from head to foot, a single farthing's worth of my own or of others. -Letter 30.

17.

They who load us with insults and ignominies give us the means of acquiring treasures more precious than any that man can gain in this life. -Letter 4.

18.

Mary's sorrow was less when she saw her

only Son crucified, that it is now at the sight of man offending Him by sin. -Nolarci.

19.

We often shut the door against the gifts and graces which God wishes to bestow on us, and show very little anxiety about keeping those He has already conferred. -Letter 34.

20.

It is better to live uncertain of salvation, and meanwhile devote one's self to the service of God and the salvation of souls, than to die at once, with the certainty of entering into everlasting glory. -Bartoli.

21.

Let us hold sacred, for the restoration of the sick, all the good things we possess; we who enjoy good health will learn, for want of better, to content ourselves with dry bread. -Bartoli, Book 3.

22.

Since we have abused the strength of body and soul to violate the law of God, we must use, after having recovered grace by repentance, this same strength to amend our lives. -Orland, Book 6, p. 1.

23.

Life would be a torment to me if I discovered, in the innermost depths of my soul, anything human or not entirely Divine. -Life, Book 4, ch. 5.

24.

It is more difficult to subdue the spirit than to mortify the flesh. -Orland.

25.

It is not enough to make profession of a kind of sublime life, if one does not fulfill perfectly all that such a state requires.
-Letter 50.

26.

When the devil suggests discouraging thoughts, we must seek help in the remembrance of the blessings, without number, that we have received from God. -Bartoli, Book 4.

27.

That he may prevent us from doing a good work, the devil often suggests a greater one; but he understands well how to prevent its execution afterwards, by new obstacles. -Discernment of Spirits.

28.

Here is the difference between a pious and a frivolous man: the first abstains from pleasure, and is overwhelmed with spiritual consolations; the other gives himself up to the pleasures of the senses, and suffers in his innermost heart. -Nolarci.

29.

Such should be our submission to the Church, that if we know visibly anything to be white, which she had declared black, we should acknowledge it black with her. -Spiritual Exercises.

30.

Never be severe in respect to those whose virtue is weak; the defiance we might arouse would produce more evil than any good results we could hope for from a severe reprimand. -Bartoli, Book 3.

OCTOBER

1.

Innocence and holiness of life are, of themselves alone, more powerful and far more preferable than all other gifts; but without prudence and the art of dealing with the world, they remain incomplete and incapable of guiding others. -Ribadeneira, ch. 37.

2.

If it seems to you that the exact point, the true medium of discretion, is difficult to find, I will tell you that you have a master to teach you, this master is obedience, whose counsels will guide you in the sure way. -Letter 50.

3.

Jesus Christ deprived Himself of His happiness, which was infinite, to make us His companions and partakers of it with Him; thus He took upon Himself our miseries to lift the burden from off our shoulders. -Letter 50.

4.

There is often more danger in making light of little faults than of great sins. -Ribadeneira, Book 5, ch. 7.

5.

How great will be your crown, if besides the obligation you are under to serve God, you add that of working for the salvation of others, and the honor and glory of God? -Letter 50.

6.

Labor to conquer yourself. This victory will assure you a brighter crown in Heaven than those gain whose disposition is more amiable. -To Edm. Anger.

7.

Paradise and eternity, are they not destined for you? When you desire to conquer them, who will prevent you? When you possess them, who will deprive you of them?
-Bartoli.

8.

Love ought to consist of deeds much more than of words. -Spiritual Exercises.

9.

Truth always shines with a brilliancy of its own, while falsehood is clouded in darkness, to dispel which it is enough to place it in the presence of truth. -Bartoli, Book 2.

10.

Should temptation assail us, are we in obscurity or sorrow, let us oppose them, without stopping at the impressions they make upon us; let us wait patiently for our Lord to console us. He will banish all trouble and dispel all darkness. -Letter 8.

11.

God desires but one thing of me, that I submit my soul to His Divine Majesty.
-Letter 9.

12.

Not only the heavens, but the sight of a blade of grass, or of the most insignificant thing, suffices to inflame with love of God the heart that knows Him. -Maffoei, Book 3. ch. 1.

13.

One might pardon, perhaps, some neglect in the service of man, but in the service of God one ought not to bear with it at any price.
-Maffoei, Book 2, ch. 3.

14.

We should confide in God, even to believing that if a vessel were wanting to us, the sea itself would afford us a safe footing.

-Maffoei.

15.

To win over the world the prudent fisher of men should be all things to all men, even though the result should not be in keeping with his efforts. -Life, Book 5, ch. 11.

16.

If one who loves God could be damned, though not through his own fault, he could more easily endure all the pains of hell than the blasphemies with which the condemned curse God. -Bartoli, Book 2.

17.

By the great love that we bear for men of decided and solid virtue, we ought to punish all the more severely the least fault in them. -Life, Book 3, n. 36.

18.

To win the good will of men in God's interest, we must be all things to all; for nothing is better calculated to win hearts than a resemblance of manners and tastes. -Nolarci

19.

God measures His love for a soul by the degree of union which exists between it and Himself, and which makes of it an apt instrument for His designs. -Bartoli, Book 1.

20.

If everything were already known and assured to us, where would be room for our confidence in God? Now we have only the shadow of these things. Where would be room for hope, if we possess them already? -Ribadeneira.

21.

We ought to place a bar on the complaints of our bodies, which, under pretense of weakness, wish to prevent us from laboring. -Bartoli, Book 5.

22.

Before choosing, let us examine well whether the attachment we feel for an object springs solely from the love of God. -Spiritual Exercises.

23.

The devil sometimes removes all fear from you, only to make you fall; he exaggerates in order to discourage you, and in everything he only seeks your ruin. -Nolarci.

24.

He who practices perfect obedience is dead to himself in order to live for God; he is not tossed here and there by his passions, but resembles a calm sea, unruffled by the tempest. -Ribadeneira, ch. 33.

25.

Who could count all those who have had wealth, power, honor? But their glory, their riches were only lent to them, and they wore themselves out in preserving and increasing that which they were forced to abandon one day. -Bartoli, Book 2.

26.

There is no need of acting niggardly, since God is so generous to us. -Letter 3.

27.

Put not off till tomorrow what you can do today, -Bartoli, Book 4.

28.

The things of this life are only really happy, as far as they prepare us for the eternal life which follows. -Bartoli,

29.

The wicked man easily suspects the virtue of others; as those who have vertigo believe that everything is turning around them.
-Maffoei.

30.

As much happiness as I felt on learning that the world had insulted you, I felt just as much pain at the single thought, that in your adversity you had sought aid and succor against the vexation and sorrow which it caused you. -Letter 4.

31.

What claims has not our Lord to our service for the blessing He has showered upon us, and which have cost Him so dear! When He proposed to sacrifice Himself because of His love for us, He forgot, it seems, according to our manner of speaking, that He was God.
-Letter 50.

NOVEMBER

1.

There is not among men, nor even among the angels, an exercise more sacred, nor a work more excellent, than to glorify God in Himself, and in creatures by bringing them to adore and serve Him as far as they are capable. -Letter 50.

2.

The unreasonable and excessive man cannot labor for any length of time in God's service; just like the steed that, running immoderately at first, gives out half way in the course, and cannot reach its destination. -Letter 50.

3.

You postpone this affair for a month, for a year! Ah! How can you count on living that length of time? -Life, Book 4, ch. 30.

4.

Love the greatest sinners; love them for the little faith they still have, or if they have none, love them for their past virtues; love God's image which they bear, love the precious Blood by which you know they have been redeemed. -Bartoli.

5.

Count as the acknowledged enemies of your soul, sloth, negligence, and idleness, which cool and weaken the desire of advancing in piety and knowledge. -Letter 50.

6.

I solemnly entreat you, in the name of our Lord and Saviour, who has not only taught us obedience by word, but also by example, to love this virtue with all your heart. -Letter on Obedience.

7.

God was pleased to ransom us, to suffer ignominy to glorify us, to choose poverty to enrich us, to die in the disgrace and agony of one condemned to secure for us everlasting life in the happiness of Heaven. -Letter 50.

8.

In certain circumstances it is better to be silent than to speak. For truth indicates itself and needs no defense. -History of the Society, Book 15, n. 44.

9.

Obedience will enable you to advance untiringly, and to gain more readily the road to Heaven; inasmuch as you will be journeying, in a manner, under the guidance of another, and not by your own will and judgment. -Letter 51.

10.

In relieving a religious of the multiplicity of personal cares, obedience not only prevents him from being irresolute and wavering, but frees him, at the same time, of the weighty responsibility of his own will; it compels him to resign all care of himself, and abandon himself entirely to the watchfulness of his superiors; from all of which is begotten peace and lasting contentment. -Letter 51.

11.

Spiritual dryness should not deject us nor consolation make us proud; in the first case we must remember the favors we have already received; and in the second not forget that it is a favor from God, which we have not merited. -Bartoli.

12.

Do not form a friendship with anyone unless you know him thoroughly. -Ribadeneira.

13.

Adversity is such, that it is really

advantageous to the just man, for it causes him a profitable loss; just as a shower of precious stones might break the leaves of the vine, but would replace them by the most beautiful treasures. -Bartoli.

14.

In revealing the defects of others we make known our own vices. -Examination.

15.

If we were to die now, what would become of us? What account could we give of all the favors and all the graces we have received, and of the many souls lost on our account? -Letters.

16.

Ah! That each day I could die a thousand cruel deaths for Christ and for the salvation of one single soul! -Life.

17.

It is better to accustom ourselves to seek God in everything we do, than to spend a long time in prayer. -Letter 95.

18.

An irresistible incentive to obedience is the loving example of the Man God, Jesus Christ, our Lord; who, while dwelling under the same roof with His parents, was subject to them; and in this Holy Family, the Virgin Mary, Queen of all, was obedient to Joseph. -Letter 51.

19.

For the love of Jesus Christ, forget the past, like St Paul, and keep your thoughts incessantly fixed on the great distance yet remaining before you reach the way of perfection. -Letter 50.

20.

He who does not love God with his whole

heart, is loving something for itself, and not for God. -Letter 3.

21.

If all things are given as a consequence to those who seek first the kingdom of God and His justice; could He fail to give something to those who seek only the justice of His Kingdom and the King of Kings Himself? -Letter 11.

22.

Should God accomplish anything great through our mediation, it should still make us count ourselves as nothing, and not cause us to take the glory to ourselves, for it does not belong to the instrument, which is often of little worth, but is due entirely to the hand which directs it. -Bartoli, Vol. 2, p. 7.

23.

In dealing with our neighbor to keep him from sinning, we ought to act with the same prudence as with a man who is drowning, so that we may avoid the danger of perishing with him. -Bartoli, Vol. 2, p. 7.

24.

Since to those who have the will nothing is difficult, above all as regards that which they would do for the love of Jesus Christ our Lord, I beseech you, then, not to make plans only, but above all to will their execution and carry them out. -Letter 3.

25.

Nothing is sweeter than to love God, but with a love rich in suffering. -Life, Book 1. n. 55.

26.

Just as I will not save myself by the good works of the angels, likewise I will not be condemned for the bad and wicked thoughts which the bad angels, the world, and the flesh present to me. -Letter 9.

27.

We must speak to God as a friend speaks to his friend, a servant to his master; now asking some favor, now acknowledging our faults, and communicating to Him all that concerns us, our thoughts, our fears, our projects, our desires, and in all things seeking His counsel. -Spiritual Exercises.

28.

There are always three sure signs of the good discipline reigning in a religious house; viz., cleanliness, strict observance of the cloister and of the rules of silence. -Lancisius.

29.

The rich ought to reach that degree of perfection of possessing the riches of which they are the masters, without allowing them to possess them. -Nolarci.

30.

When you behold complete prosperity reigning anywhere, you may ask yourself if the service of God is not neglected there.
-Life, Book 5., ch. 11.

DECEMBER

1.

Discretion is necessary in spiritual life; it is its part to restrain the exercises in the way of perfection, so as to keep us between the two extremes. -Letter 50.

2.

Those whose circumstances in the world would have assured them an ample fortune, labor in religion with the greater success in promoting the glory of God. -Bartoli, Book 1. ch. 1.

3.

Do not think that you injure spiritual progress is that which you grant to the needs of nature. -History of the Society, Book 1. p. 1.

4.

They who are working for the salvation of souls, ought to seek God's friendship, then man's for God, and regulate their zeal for the honor of God by the advancement of their neighbor. -Bartoli.

5.

Resolve never to do anything while moved by passion; wait until it passes away and then take counsel only after mature deliberation. -Of the Elect.

6.

Oh my God! Oh God infinitely good! How can You bear with a sinner like me! -Ribadeneira.

7.

If you follow neither rule nor measure, you turn the good into evil, virtue into vice. -Spiritual Exercises.

8.

It is necessary to destroy anything which is good in itself because of its abuses; that would be to impede the work which ought to largely increase the glory of God. -Gonzal. de Cam.

9.

In leaving God for God, there is a great spiritual gain and nothing to lose. -Bartoli, Book 4.

10.

As God is not the only witness of our life, but as moreover the world, the angels and men behold it, let us be good not only before God, but also before men. -Ribadeneira.

11.

We must praise God in His Saints, as the Psalmist tells us. -Letter 3.

12.

Obedience is a guide which cannot err, an interpreter of the Divine Will, which cannot deceive. -Summary of Constitutions.

13.

The greatest reward that a servant of God can receive for that which he has done for his neighbor is scorn or contempt, the only reward that the world gave for the labors of its Divine Master. -Bartoli, Vol. 2, p. 7.

14.

Truth always ends by victory; it is not unassailable, but invincible. -Nolarci.

15.

If the enemy exalts us, we must humble ourselves, recalling our sins and our miseries; if he humbles and degrades us, we must rise ourselves by a true faith and hope in our Lord, remembering the blessing received from Him and considering how, with infinite love and burning heart, He waits to save us. -Letter 8.

16.

If God gives you much suffering, it is a sign that He wishes to make you a great Saint. -Bartoli, Book 4.

17.

May the holy name of our Lord be ever blessed; may it be eternally praised by every creature, who has been created and placed in this world only for that end, so just in itself and so lawfully imposed. -Letter 33.

18.

The value of a thing is only its worth before God. -Bartoli, Book 4, ch. 55.

19.

One cannot be the friend of Jesus Christ, without loving the souls He has redeemed with His precious Blood. -Nolarci.

20.

They who wish to do great things in the service of their Lord and King, will not rest with mere deeds; but will also wage war against their sensuality, their carnal and worldly love, and will thus make offerings to Him of the highest value. -Spiritual Exercises.

21.

A bow breaks if it is bent too much, but the soul is lost if it relaxes itself. -Letter 50.

22.

We are not the masters of our bodies; God is; therefore we cannot all practice corporal mortification in the same degree. -Bartoli, Book 4, p. 381.

23.

We no sooner begin a work for the honor and glory of God, than the world at once becomes uneasy, or the devil throws obstacles in the way. -Nolarci.

24.

Should there be no lurking evils in a house where peace and tranquility reign, it is all that can be desired, it is everything. -Bartoli, Book 3. s

25.

Last Christmas day, I had the happiness of saying my first Mass in the Church of St Mary Major, in the chapel where the crib of the Infant Jesus is. -Letter 14.

26.

He lives happily who, unceasingly, as far as he is able, has his mind on God and God in his heart. -Life, Book 3, n. 1.

27.

Let us serve God; He will certainly take care of us and we shall want for nothing. -Ribadeneira.

28.

You wish to reform the world, reform yourself, otherwise your efforts will be in vain. -Bartoli, Book 4.

29.

It is better to be cut off from life, than to live for vanity. -Nolarci.

30.

Do not wait for old age to mortify your body and your passions. First, are you sure of reaching it? Again, how shall you do penance at that age? -Nolarci.

31.

He who by nature is coarse and violent, and who by dint of resolution becomes gentle and amiable, often becomes capable of great and difficult undertakings in the service of God; because of that very stubbornness, or that natural obstinacy, used in a good cause, knows neither defeat nor discouragement.
-Bartoli, Book 4.

OTHER TITLES OFFERED BY
ST ATHANASIUS PRESS
http://www.stathanasiuspress.com

Be sure to check our web site for the newest Titles being offered and for our latest contact information!

The 1957 Edition of The Raccolta
or A Manual of Indulgences

Vera Sapentia or True Wisdom
by Thomas A Kempis

Treatise on Prayer
by St Alphonsus Liguori

3 Volume Set
The Practice of Christian and Religious Perfection
by Fr Alphonsus Rodriguez, S.J.

The Eternal Happiness of the Saints
by St Robert Bellarmine

Devotion to the Nine Choirs of Holy Angels
by Henri-Marie Boudon

The Valley of Lilies & The Little Garden of Roses
by Thomas A Kempis

A Thought From Thomas A Kempis
for Each Day of the Year

The History of Heresies and Their Refutation
by St Alphonsus Liguori

1910 Benziger Catalog - Fully Illustrated
Church Ornaments of Our Own Manufacture

The Spiritual Conflict and Conquest
by Dom Juan Castiniza, O.S.B.

St Alphonsus Liguori on the Council of Trent

Dignity and Duties of the Priest or Selva
by St Alphonsus Liguori

The Maxims and Sayings of St Philip Neri

The Triumph of the Cross
by Savonarola

Indifferentism
or Is One Religion as Good as Another?

Explanation of the Psalms and Canticles
in the Divine Office
by St Alphonsus Liguori

Collection of Catholic Prayers and Devotions
based on the 1957 Raccolta

The Holy Ways of the Cross
by Henri-Marie Boudon

www.ingramcontent.com/pod-product-compliance
Lightning Source LLC
LaVergne TN
LVHW041630070426
835507LV00008B/548